LAURA BUSH

OTHER BOOKS BY LOUANN ATKINS TEMPLE IN THE BIOGRAPHY FOR BEGINNING HISTORIANS SERIES

Barbara Bush

George W. Bush

Lyndon B. Johnson

George H. W. Bush

Lady Bird Johnson

LAURA BUSH

A Biography for Beginning Historians

LOUANN ATKINS TEMPLE

THE LBJ FOUNDATION

Distributed by the University of Texas Press

First edition, 2025

♾ The paper used in this book meets the minimum requirements of ANSI/NISO Z39.48-1992 (R1997) (Permanence of Paper).

Library of Congress Control Number: 2025936898

ISBN 978-1-4773-3211-5 (paperback)
ISBN 978-1-4773-3212-2 (PDF)
ISBN 978-1-4773-3213-9 (ePub)

doi:10.7560/332115

To Ashley, with love

When asked who her role model would be in the White House, Laura replied, "I think I'll just be Laura Bush."

CONTENTS

LAURA BUSH

INTRODUCTION

In this book, you will not read about every trip Laura Bush took. There are too many. Every cause she initiated and worked on. Way too many. Every occasion she hosted or attended. An endless number. But I do hope to make you aware of the energy and devotion that led to her almost endless action on behalf of her country.

Laura Bush did not seek recognition. She sought only to help: first with the education of women and children, then boys, especially those outside of the United States, who had been in prison or had troubled lives. Her later works expanded to include almost anyone whose lives could be made better through her contributions.

The pace of her life as First Lady has been breathtaking. It is also dismaying to know how many threats there were to her and her family's safety. It is hard to imagine how President George W. Bush, in spite of his strengths, could have made it through the difficulties of his years in office without the equal strengths of Laura Bush.

She is an unheralded hero for all these reasons.

CHAPTER 1

GROWING UP AND GOING TO COLLEGE

Laura Welch was born November 4, 1946, in a distinctive part of the country—West Texas—that tends to give its children a pioneer mentality of adventurousness and strength against all odds. These traits predominated in her along with gentleness and a caring heart.

She was an only child in a family where four children had been born, but only she, the second one, had survived infancy.

Midland, a town of about nine thousand people during the 1950s, offered a stable childhood. Her family liked to laugh, had cats and dogs and parakeets and turtles and horny toads, and they ate together three times a day (fresh vegetables, nothing out of a can). She dutifully set the table and made her bed and was paid five cents if she made coffee in the morning for her mother and father. Her mother read *Snow White* and *Little Women* to her.

In those days, no one locked their doors, children could roam the streets freely, television broadcast only in the late afternoon and early evening hours, families took driving trips, and high school football reigned on Friday nights. The recent World War II was not mentioned, as if it had not happened, something to forget. Laura's handsome father, Harold Welch, had gone to college for two years at Texas Tech University and had fought in the war. After the war, he would not own a gun, which was unusual in West Texas. He did other West Texas things: followed football passionately and played craps and the card game gin rummy for money. He worked as district manager for a loan company and traveled frequently. On the side, he built and sold new houses.

Laura's mother, Jenna Hawkins Welch, from El Paso, had attended college at what is now the University of Texas at El Paso, but she did not stay long enough to earn a degree. At the age of six, Laura was allowed to make the six-hour train trip alone to El Paso to visit her grandparents.

Also at six, Laura was diagnosed with progressive myopia, which restricted her eyesight. When she was fitted with glasses, she saw the outline of objects for the first time in her life.

Laura learned early that she loved teaching. She taught swimming at the Midland public pool and worked as a counselor at summer camps. Before that, she taught her dolls, setting up a schoolroom for them at home in her bedroom. Other pastimes were taking ballet and piano lessons.

George W. lived only ten blocks away from Laura, but they did not know each other and did not meet until they were thirty-one.

In high school, she loved her classwork and made good grades. Girls in Midland did not tend to drink, but they did smoke. They listened to Elvis and the Beatles, and their idea of excitement was to sneak out of the house at night in their pajamas and walk down the street together.

Laura Welch's senior yearbook photo from Robert E. Lee High School, Midland, Texas, around 1964. Courtesy of George W. Bush Presidential Library.

Then, one night changed her life. In 1963, just after her seventeenth birthday, she and a friend were going out. They decided to drive by the theater to see what movie was playing. Laura was driving a heavy Chevy Impala, and moving at less than the speed limit. She did not see the stop sign at one intersection until it was too late. She ran the stop sign and hit a small, compact Corvair Monza coming from the other street. Laura was thrown from the car and hit her head and rolled in the grass. Apparently, the car door had been flung open by the impact. (This was just before seat belts became standard in cars in 1964.) Laura's face was bruised, she had a gash on her knee, and her ankle was broken. As she lay there, she heard the police and ambulance sirens wailing as they drew near. Just before she was taken to the hospital emergency room, she spotted Mr. Douglas, her friend Mike's father, as he bent over the other car. Mike, too, was taken to the hospital emergency room but sadly passed away. Laura could hear Mike's parents sobbing over the loss of their child. He had been a handsome athlete and her good friend, with whom she had talked for hours on the phone; they had the same circle of friends.

Already, that year, two other people had been killed at that same intersection. The city subsequently installed a much larger stop sign and warning signs at that spot.

The next morning Laura's parents went to see Mike Douglas's parents. Laura never knew what words were exchanged between them. Her parents decided it would be best if Laura did not attend the funeral, and no one ever mentioned the tragedy again. Today she still feels the guilt she felt so strongly that night, and now she realizes that she should have gone to see his parents and that she should have kept in contact with them.

In her autobiography, she bravely tells this story in detail. Through the years, she has received many requests from strangers to write to a young person in similar circumstances, which she always does, telling them to talk with people they love and get professional help. She tells them that, although they will never get over what happened, they can move on.

Laura's parents insisted that she attend college. She chose Southern Methodist University (SMU) in Dallas. In those days, curfew for girls in dormitories was ten o'clock on weekdays and midnight on weekends. Girls had to wear dresses or skirts that covered the knee to class. Many of her classmates were more interested in finding a husband than in earning a degree, but because Laura knew she wanted to become a teacher, she became a serious student after her first semester, in which she said her grades were "embarrassing." After graduating in 1968, becoming only the second person in her family to earn a degree, Laura took some time to tour Europe with relatives before returning to Texas to begin her career.

CHAPTER 2

ADULT LIFE BEFORE GEORGE

Laura knew she wanted to teach in a school serving minority populations. Her first job was as a fourth grade teacher in the wealthy Highland Park suburb of Dallas. She rented an apartment two blocks from the school. She didn't drive if she could help it. The twenty students in her class were mostly African Americans who were bused in from another part of town because Highland Park residents tended to send their children to private schools. Laura said the experience was "deeply rewarding."

By the end of the school year, she was restless and ready to leave Texas. She and a friend drove to Boston to look for work. After three days there, they decided to try Washington, DC, instead. When she couldn't find work she wanted, she left her friend and drove alone back to Texas and to Houston. She got a job in a stock brokerage business but said, "I was dreadfully bored and longed to return to the classroom." Teaching was her love.

She taught fourth grade in Houston to a wild, disobedient group of youngsters. The next year she moved to second grade and, the year after that, to third grade.

Outside school, she and her friends sailed in the Ship Channel, took weekend trips to Galveston, Mexico and Austin, and cooked King Ranch chicken (chicken, canned mushroom soup, tomatoes, and chiles in a casserole) for dinner guests.

Laura looked for a new challenge after those years, and applied to the library science program at the University of Texas at Austin. There, she settled into an apartment with a kitten she named Dewey, after the Dewey decimal system. Happily, she spent her days at the campus's Harry Ransom Center, surrounded by Shakespeare's First Folio of manuscripts, John Keats's poems, and hundreds of other originals from world literature. This was the life she wanted.

While she was in school, President Lyndon Johnson died. As Laura walked by his coffin, while he was lying in honor at the LBJ Library on the UT campus, she got to shake hands with Lady Bird Johnson, never dreaming that she, too, would someday serve as First Lady.

Laura received her master's degree in library science and returned to Houston. This time, she worked in a library. But Austin called to her, and she decided to return once again, this time as a school librarian at Mollie Dawson Elementary, located in a largely Hispanic neighborhood. Now she was thirty, settled down, teaching, driving to Midland to see her parents, and going with friends to hear music at Austin's famed Armadillo World Headquarters.

CHAPTER 3

MARRIAGE AND POLITICS

Meanwhile, George W. Bush was working in Midland as a landman (one who negotiates with landowners to acquire leases) in the oil business. He and Laura had mutual friends, Jan and Joey O'Neill, who wanted them to meet. Laura was in no rush because she knew he was interested in politics and she was not. But one night when Laura was in Midland, the O'Neills had Laura and George over for hamburgers. "We laughed and talked until it was nearly midnight," she remembered. The next day George called and asked her to play miniature golf. Then he began visiting her in Austin. Within mere months, he had asked her to marry him. She said yes. Laura remembers that when she met him, "I loved how he made me laugh and his steadfastness. I knew in my heart that he was the one."

Only a week after proposing, George invited Laura to Houston, and introduced her to his parents with the news that they were engaged.

They set a date in three weeks for a wedding in Midland. They wanted it to be simple. Laura's mother wrote all the wedding invitations by hand since there was not enough time to have them printed. There would be seventy-five guests but no bridesmaids or groomsmen. Laura chose an ivory silk skirt and blouse. She carried a bouquet of gardenias and wore gardenias in her hair.

The night before the wedding, George stood to toast Laura at the rehearsal dinner in the new Hilton Hotel and wept. His equally sentimental father didn't even try to give a toast because he knew that he would have teared up too. His mother Barbara had to do it for them.

The wedding was held on a Saturday morning in 1977 at the First Methodist Church, followed by a wedding lunch of chicken and rice at the Racquet Club. Barbara Bush and Jenna Welch had not thought to compare menus. Chicken and rice had also been served at the Hilton the night before.

For their honeymoon, Laura and George chose Cozumel, Mexico, where they drove the length of the island in a rented car, saw iguanas everywhere, sat on the beach, drank margaritas, and played gin rummy. They returned home to a newly purchased house by the golf course in Midland.

Now they faced the problems of daily living. Laura learned that George loved to talk and could be boisterous, that he dropped his wet towels on the furniture, and was not a great handyman. And, yes, he was well into politics. Before they married, he had decided to run for US Congress. George's father had helped build the Republican Party in Midland, a city that tended to vote solidly Democratic for all offices except president. Laura said it was a "What the heck, why not" run for George. They hit the campaign trail, covering a wide swath of West Texas in George's Oldsmobile.

This was her introduction to campaigning. At her request, George promised she would never have to make a speech. She said that was the only promise he ever made to her that he

George W. Bush and Laura Welch at their wedding, Midland, Texas, November 1977. Courtesy of George H. W. Bush Presidential Library and Museum.

broke. One night she had to represent him at a town meeting when he had a conflict, and there she made her first speech, at which time she realized that standing before a classroom of children had prepared her well for standing before adults. She had actually enjoyed the event.

George said that "Laura was a natural campaigner. Her genuineness made it easy for voters to relate to her."

George won the primary. He faced Democrat Kent Hance in the general election, and lost by only 6 percent of the vote. "We were sad," said Laura, "but not disappointed."

George turned to business. He formed a company to do oil exploration and set out to find investors. One night they were dining at 21 Club in New York with prospective investors when the waiter rolled a TV over to their table, and they watched the surprise announcement that candidate Ronald Reagan had just chosen George H. W. Bush as his vice presidential running mate. George and Laura rushed to the Republican National Convention in Detroit and immediately began helping his dad with his campaign. They were back in politics. Reagan-Bush won in a landslide. Laura and George were in Washington for the inauguration.

George began his oil exploration company with seven employees, calling it Arbusto, which is Spanish for "bush." After building his company to a successful and profitable operation, he sold it by merging it with another company.

In the midst of their bustling business life and political life, they were eager to become parents. They had been married nearly four years and decided to apply to the Gladney Home in Fort Worth to adopt a child. Soon, though, Laura learned that she was pregnant. She and George cried with joy when the doctor told them that they were having twins.

When the girls—Barbara, named after George's mother, and Jenna, named after Laura's mother—were born, George sent a dozen roses to Laura's hospital room containing a card that said, "With love, from the father of twins."

Laura would later refer to those early mornings, when she and George each held a baby while they drank coffee and read the news in bed, as "some of the sweetest times in our lives."

Both girls were early talkers. Their first word was *Daddy.* George loved being a dad; he changed diapers and got up at night to help feed them, and, as they got older, played games with them.

On Fridays, he and Laura usually ate Mexican food and drank margaritas. On Saturdays, they often had dinner at a friend's house. Drinking was a regular part of social life in Midland. One day, George decided he had had enough. Drinking was not helping him to be the man, husband, and father he wanted to be. He stopped and was surprised at how quickly he felt better when he awoke in the morning and throughout the whole day.

When George H. W. Bush decided to run for president, he asked George W. to move to Washington to help with his campaign. Laura, in 1988, realized that, at age forty-one, she had never lived outside Texas for more than a few weeks, and more than twenty-five of those years had been in Midland. Their move to Washington marked a time when that Laura and her mother-in-law finally got to know each other well, and the children got to know their paternal grandparents.

George H. W. won the election and became president of the United States.

In 1988, the Texas Rangers baseball team came up for sale.

The Bush family (*left to right:* Jenna, George, Laura, and Barbara Bush), Kennebunkport, Maine, August 1990. Courtesy of George H. W. Bush Presidential Library and Museum.

Suddenly, Laura and George and the girls were moving to Dallas while George and a friend put together a group of investors to buy the club. Once the purchase was successful, Laura and George realized how much fun they could have—they could be found in the stands for nearly all of their team's home games.

They bought a house in Dallas and settled in with occasional trips to Washington to participate in White House life. Then, in 1992, Bill Clinton defeated President Bush and became president himself. A new thought captured George W. Bush—he would run for governor of Texas. At the same time, his brother Jeb decided to run for governor of Florida. Politics, it seemed, was the Bush family business. Pursuing his new goal, George W. launched his campaign in 1994 against popular incumbent Democratic Governor Ann Richards.

The race forced Laura to live a double life as wife of the candidate and mother of two twelve-year-olds. She flew around the state campaigning in the daytime and tried to be home for dinner with the girls at night. George won his race, but brother Jeb in Florida lost his. The family left Dallas and moved into the Governor's Mansion in Austin, where Jenna and Barbara spent their high school years, having sleepovers with their friends in the Sam Houston bedroom and being driven to school in a limousine by Department of Public Safety agents.

On that first Inauguration Day, Laura's father was battling skin cancer from his life in the sun, as well as dementia, and he was unable to share the day with the Bush family. Only her mother could be there. Several months later, her father died.

From the very beginning, Laura and George made education reform and enhancement a focus of their political life. Laura held a national conference in Austin on early childhood development and brain research, helping to persuade legislators to create reading readiness programs and add funds to the Head Start program. She also supported caseworkers who cared for abandoned and abused children, and who often spent their own money to get the children essential items like pajamas and diapers.

At the suggestion of a writer in the Capitol who said she

was the perfect person to start one, she organized the Texas Book Festival. The first festival was held in the Capitol and in tents nearby. She was so afraid it would be a failure that on the first day she went to bed instead of going to the event. But her friends told her what a success the programs were, so she got out of bed and went to the Capitol with them. Fifteen thousand people attended that first festival, and over its first fourteen seasons, it gave over $2.3 million to Texas libraries. It is still held each fall in Austin.

On George's fiftieth birthday, Laura threw a surprise party for him, at which the Democratic lieutenant governor, Bob Bullock, toasted George as "the next president of the United States."

CHAPTER 4

THE PRESIDENCY

George did run for president, but Laura was less than enthusiastic because she knew how mean politics could be. "I believed in my George," she said, "I love him, and I knew he would be a great president. It was the process in which I had far less faith." And, of course, it meant they would be away from home and their daughters most of the time. They missed the surprise announcement of Barbara being crowned homecoming queen at Austin High School because they were on the campaign trail. Laura did take time off from campaigning to help Jenna move into her dorm at the University of Texas and Barbara into her dorm at Yale.

When George debated his democratic opponent, Al Gore, he was behind in the polls. After three debates, he was ahead. But they went into Election Day in a dead heat because five days earlier, the story broke that George had, years prior, been arrested for driving while intoxicated.

Laura and George voted in Austin and then awaited election returns with their family at the Governor's Mansion. The news media said the election was too close to call. It was another thirty-five days before the Supreme Court, by a 5–4 vote in a landmark case, finally declared George the winner.

As a result, there were only four weeks for Laura to get ready for her husband's inauguration as president of the United States. She chose clothes for inaugural events, toured the White House with First Lady Hillary Clinton, packed, moved to Washington, and even found time to plan and hold her own event on the eve of the inauguration, which featured authors and celebrated books and reading. That night, George introduced her to the crowd, saying, "Her love for books is real, her love for children is real, and my love for her is real."

On the cold and rainy inaugural day, Laura and George attended services at St. John's Episcopal Church, then went to the White House for coffee with the Clintons and the Gores. The traditional motorcade began down Pennsylvania Avenue with the two presidents leading and the two First Ladies following in the car behind. George took his oath of office with his hand on the same Bush family Bible his father had used.

The swearing-in was followed by a lunch in the Capitol and a parade featuring bands and floats from every state, including the SMU and University of Texas bands.

At each inaugural ball that night, they were introduced onstage, danced a bit, waved goodbye, and went on to the next. They were home before midnight to their 132-room, fifty-five-thousand-square-foot house with twenty-three relatives sleeping in the bedrooms. Already, the staff had moved the Clintons' clothes and furniture out and the Bushes' in. They had even put toothpaste and toothbrushes on the bathroom counters. Laura drifted off to sleep "knowing that everyone we loved was safe, tucked in together under this one, remarkable roof."

The inaugural prayer service the next morning at the Na-

President and Mrs. Bush board *Air Force One*, June 2001. As First Lady, Mrs. Bush traveled to all fifty American states and visited more than seventy-five countries. Courtesy of George W. Bush Presidential Library.

tional Cathedral ended with the singing of "America the Beautiful." The Bushes ate brunch with friends, and then George went to the Oval Office and Laura to her own office in the East Wing of the White House. Their presidency began.

Laura soon learned that she needed clothes for many occasions, including gowns for state dinners, and a hairdresser, and countless personal expenses like their food and White House Christmas parties. Clothes, especially, presented problems for the not-too-fashion-minded Laura. Just before one interview, Laura realized that she had worn the same clothes for their previous interview with her, and she had to swap blouses with her press secretary.

Right away Laura became honorary chair of Save America's Treasures, an organization that works to to protect the country's historic sites and possessions. She began arranging rooms in the White House to include many of these treasures. (Simultaneously, she was flying to Texas to oversee the building of their house in Crawford).

She soon began her educational initiatives by visiting schools to highlight her planned programs, which included holding an early childhood cognitive development conference, trying to encourage more retired military to go into teaching, and advertising the Teach for America program more widely.

She also began seriously considering a national book festival.

In addition to all this, endless trips and events filled Laura and George's time. They flew to Italy for an audience with the pope and to England, where they had dinner with Queen Elizabeth and Prince Philip at Buckingham Palace. They also held their first state dinner for President Vicente Fox of Mexico.

The White House was preparing for a Texas-style cookout on the lawn for over one thousand people to honor the members of Congress. It was September 11, the day that informally has been named 9/11. The morning started out sunny and warm. George was in Florida visiting a school. Laura was on the way to the Capitol with Democratic Senator Ted

Kennedy to testify before the Senate Education Committee. They heard the news on the radio. A commercial airline plane had crashed into the World Trade Center in New York. Soon, they learned that a plane had also crashed in Pennsylvania and another at the Pentagon. The White House was ordered to evacuate, and the Secret Service whisked Laura to a safe underground place in one of their buildings, where she watched a replay on television of 1,500 people and 110 stories of building crash to the ground. A week later, the initial estimates of those killed in the World Trade Center buildings passed six thousand.

In the meantime, Secret Service agents had collected Barbara and Jenna at their schools and taken them to safe sites. Laura tried to call George and couldn't get through. At the same time, on *Air Force One*, George was trying unsuccessfully to call her. Finally, they made contact, and she told him that the girls and the White House staff were safe. Someone went to the White House and got clothes for Laura and even brought her their two dogs, Barney and Spot, and their cat, Kitty.

By nightfall, George had arrived in Washington, and the family was sequestered in a secret underground part of the White House. The Presidential Emergency Operations Center came complete with steel doors. When bedtime came, Laura and George decided they wanted to sleep in their own bed and went back upstairs with the dogs and the cat. During the night, someone ran into the room, shouting, "Mr. President, Mr. President, you've got to get up! The White House is under attack!" Once more they ran to the underground hideaway, carrying one dog and the cat, with the other dog running along behind. It was a false alarm. After that, fighter planes cruised low over the White House every night so there would be no more alarms.

When Laura woke up the morning following the 9/11 attacks, she said, "I saw George, and I knew, knew that yesterday would be with us, each day, for all of our days to come."

That morning Laura went to Walter Reed Army Medical Center and spoke to many of the injured from the Pentagon and to the doctors and nurses. And, of course, she thought of the nation's children. She wrote two letters, one to older children and the other to younger ones, which were read nationwide on television, telling them that this was their opportunity to think of others and to help by being kind and showing love. She attended memorial services at the National Cathedral and in Pennsylvania. In Pennsylvania, she said to the families, "The loved ones we remember today knew—even in those horrible moments—that they were not truly alone, because your love was with them." Everywhere she went, people gave her mementos of their lost loved ones, all of which she and George saved. One such memento was a picture of a twenty-five-year-old girl, handed to Laura by the girl's mother, which she tucked into the mirror frame of her bureau in the White House and looked at every day. She invited family members of the victims of the Pennsylvania crash to the White House to hear their stories. She encouraged three thousand members of Learning Leaders in New York to see that their schools were soon reopened. She visited the school closest to the Twin Towers, in which the children, holding hands, had watched the towers falling and crumbling, then ran for their lives a mile and a half to another school.

Laura recalled in a memoir that her and George's comfort through those days was in just knowing they were both in the same room together. "We are anchored to each other."

Twenty-six days after 9/11, the president announced military action against Afghanistan because the Taliban had ignored his ultimatum to turn over Osama bin Laden, who was responsible for the attacks. American and British aircraft dropped bombs on the country to combat the terrorists. They also dropped food, medicine, and transistor radios for the Afghan people's welfare.

Soon poisoned letters containing powdered anthrax began arriving at newscasters' offices, in the Senate, and in government mail rooms. Several workers died. The White House was quarantined and mail delivery there cut off. Tourists were not allowed on the grounds or in the house. Instead, bomb-sniffing dogs and sharpshooters made the rounds. Five weeks later, after no new threats, life returned to a kind of normality, and Laura was allowed to travel again. She toured the country, conducting classes for Teach for America to highlight their services to the country. In Houston, a little girl snuggled up to her and asked, "What did you think about what happened?" Laura replied, "I'm sad." "I'm sad, too," said the child. Laura addressed women throughout the world by radio, and wherever she went, women thanked her.

George was asked to throw the first pitch in a World Series game that fall, and Laura sat in fear as he walked alone out to the mound with no agents around him and the stands packed. She smiled in relief when he threw a strike and the crowd began chanting "USA! USA! USA!" in approbation.

Laura was asked to light the Rockefeller Center Christmas tree in New York City to honor the lost loved ones of 9/11. New York, which had seen nothing but empty streets and armed guards since the attack, came to life momentarily when she switched on the light. The tree's five miles' worth of bulbs—thirty thousand reds, whites, and blues—brought

Laura Bush poses with children at the National Book Festival, Library of Congress, Washington, DC, September 2001. Courtesy of George W. Bush Presidential Library.

cheers and applause from the hundred thousand people in the streets waiting for it to tell them that New York was alive again.

In Washington, that year the only way people were able to see the White House Christmas decorations was when Laura, with Barney and Spot wagging their tails beside her, gave a televised tour through the decorated house. Laura said that Kitty "refused to mug for the camera."

Laura quit watching TV and turned to books for comfort. And she looked for ways to comfort others. She began hosting a series of videos celebrating American authors, and she saw that aid was sent to Afghanistan, everything from coats to soap to toys. She and George created America's Fund for Afghan Children, asking children in the US to join them by making contributions of a dollar. In less than four years, they received millions of dollars in contributions.

One weekend, when George was out of the country, Laura went to their ranch in Texas. After dinner the first night, Secret Service agents appeared in the dining room to tell her that they had learned of an attack planned on the ranch. She and her dinner guest sat in the dark all night, fearing an assault that never came. A number of similar threats occurred in the coming months, including a national terrorist alert at a nuclear facility.

On the first anniversary of 9/11, the priest who preached the sermon at St. John's Episcopal Church across the square from the White House said that 9/11 was like "a tattoo on our national soul," marking us "indelibly and forever."

For the next six years, each year on 9/11, on the White House South Lawn, at precisely 8:46 a.m., the Bushes, along with White House staff and the Cabinet, bowed their heads for a moment of silence to remember those who had been lost. At final count, 2,973 innocent people died that morning.

Laura spoke at the Smithsonian Museum's opening of an exhibit to commemorate 9/11 on its first anniversary. Included were such items as a crowbar found next to the body of a firefighter, boots and helmets of rescuers, the bullhorn the president had shouted through just days after the attack, when he said to New Yorkers, "I can hear you! The rest of the world hears you! And the people who knocked these buildings down will hear all of us soon." One exhibit wall displayed prayers and pictures of loved ones who were missing during the fire and it's aftermath.

On that first anniversary, President Bush spoke to the United Nations and obtained a resolution from the group that brought Iraq into the equation. He announced that Saddam Hussein was thought to have weapons of mass destruction that Iraq must reveal and destroy. Global intelligence suggested that chemical or biological weapons could be used in another attack. President Bush made a decision he had hoped never to have to make. He sent the American military to war against Iraq. Along with forty other nations, the US bombed the country and sent in ground troops. Every day, the president read the casualty reports. He wrote personal letters to families whose loved ones had died in Iraq.

In the next months, at home, horrible events alternated with satisfying ones. Sniper attacks occurred on the streets from time to time. One sniper, when he was caught, confessed that the aim of the killings had been eventually to extort money from the government so that he could "set up a camp to train children how to terrorize cities." One rumor even stated that a plane had hit the Bush ranch in Crawford, Texas.

Laura continued to find ways to help children get a good education. She formed the Military Child Education Coalition with governors' wives to allow children whose parents were in the military to move from state to state and take their academic standing with them. She worked for the arts, hosting a symposium on Mark Twain and an event to highlight the Harlem Renaissance, then one on women writers of the American West and another on Southern writers. Some scholars refused to come because they disagreed politically with the president's actions in Iraq.

The political turmoil caused by going to war even invaded the Bushes' daughters' classrooms. Barbara called home to tell Laura that the teaching assistant in one of her classes at Yale had told her, "I'll give you an A if your dad doesn't go to war in Iraq." Barbara bypassed the teaching aid after that and submitted her coursework directly to her professor. Laura discovered repeatedly that her earlier fear about the sometimes meanness of politics was well founded.

Two years had passed since 9/11. The Iraq War continued. The third National Book Festival was held. Queen Elizabeth and Prince Philip hosted Laura and George at Buckingham Palace. George made a secret trip to Iraq at Thanksgiving and served Thanksgiving dinner to the soldiers in the chow line. The Bushes held a Christmas party for children around Washington whose parents were serving in the military. Then, on December 13, Saddam Hussein, the leader of Iraq during the Iraq War, was found hiding in a hole. He was captured, tried, convicted, and executed by his own country.

The next year was an election year. George would be running for president for the second and the last time. Laura campaigned across the country, taking "strength and solace" from the tens of thousands of people who cheered her along the way. When Jenna and Barbara graduated from college, they came home to live and to work within the presidential campaign, first answering the telephone at campaign headquarters and, later, going out on the campaign trail to make speeches themselves. Along the way, Jenna met another campaign worker, named Henry Hager, who would become her husband.

Their hard work paid off. George won reelection over his opponent, John Kerry, by more than three million votes.

After years of anticipation, Laura embarked on a trip to

Afghanistan in 2005, which she planned in secret for safety reasons. She decided to attend the US-Afghan Women's Council, a women-led partnership designed to enable Afghan women to open businesses, secure an education, and begin to assume leadership roles. Laura arrived in the decimated city of Kabul, which had no electricity and was full of rubble and bombed-out buildings. Children there even wandered the streets without wearing shoes or coats. Her visit surprised and delighted participants of the council. She gave a speech announcing the establishment of the American University of Afghanistan and the International School of Kabul, which was a high school. At the end of that day, Laura ate with the American troops, then was soon on an airplane headed back to Andrews Air Force Base outside Washington.

A few days later, she was headed to Rome for the funeral of Pope John Paul II. A month later, she spoke in Amman, Jordan, as UNESCO's honorary ambassador for its Decade of Literacy and had dinner with their king and queen. During her speech, some of the men from Saudi Arabia walked out in disapproval of her message on behalf of women. On her way to the airport, a car forced its way into her convoy. Secret Service surrounded her with shouldered guns and intercepted the car. She never knew what kind of threat it had presented. More undefined scares awaited her in Israel and in Egypt, making her more thankful than ever for her relatively safe American life and the pleasure Americans take in making fun of themselves.

The organizers of the White House Correspondents' Dinner asked her to speak before three thousand people, parodying the president, as they did every year at their black-tie gathering before a room full of celebrities. Laura said she was close to petrified when she started, but she soon had the room laughing uproariously. By plan, she interrupted George just as he had started to make a speech to the assembly. "I've got a few things I want to say for a change," she began. Looking surprised, he sat down, and she took the podium. She poked light fun at her husband, saying, "George always says he's 'delighted' to come to these press dinners. Baloney. He's usually in bed by now. . . . George, if you really want to end tyranny in the world, you're going to have to stay up later." The speech received a standing ovation. She ended it on a sweet note. "So, in the future, when you see me just quietly sitting up here, I want you to know I'm happy to be here for a reason: I love and enjoy being with the man who usually speaks to you on these occasions."

In 2005, Laura and daughter Jenna made a trip to South Africa, where Laura's other daughter, Barbara, was working in Cape Town at the Red Cross War Memorial Children's Hospital, which treated AIDS. About 70 percent of the world's AIDS cases are in Africa. Laura and Jenna were there as part of the Mothers2Mothers program, which helps women deal with AIDS in their and their children's lives. They heard many tragic stories about the disease: women whose families had disowned them or whose husbands had left them because they had AIDS, large families in which every member of the family had the disease, and children who were raising themselves because both of their parents had died from it. Laura and Jenna continued on to Tanzania, to Zanzibar, and to Rwanda on the same mission. In Zanzibar, they also celebrated the gift made by American public and private organizations of twenty thousand books for children to read. Laura said that she had been changed by going to Africa because of the "tremendous hope I have seen among its people in the midst of overwhelming despair."

In 2005, Hurricane Katrina crossed Florida and moved across the Gulf of Mexico, before making final impact in Louisiana. More than one million people were without power as winds roared at 155 miles per hour, sixteen inches of rain fell, and levees in New Orleans gave way. The Coast Guard had to rescue more than thirty-three thousand people. The president flew over New Orleans, which was being evacuated, but did not land because he did not want to divert a single rescue worker from doing their job. However, he and Laura did go to other Southern cities to talk to people who had evacuated their homes. The Red Cross, Salvation Army, Southern Baptist Convention, and thousands of volunteers from across the country appeared to help, cooking thousands of meals each day and gathering clothes for families who had lost everything. Volunteers helped parents find their toddlers from whom they had been separated. First responders treated the sick and injured. Thousands donated blood. Former sheriffs and Secret Service agents looked for the missing. Within six months, children were reunited with their families. Dogs and cats by the hundreds were flown to shelters, and many of them were eventually reunited with their owners. The others were adopted. Laura traveled the South, visiting with those who had lost their homes and towns. She saw to it that money was raised throughout the country, and within a few months books had been given to 428 school libraries. Eventually, $6 million was raised to rebuild the library collections in devastated schools.

Laura hosted Lady Bird Johnson at the White House in the fall of 2005. Laura had met Lady Bird during her graduate school years in Austin but never dreamed they would someday meet again with Lady Bird as a guest in Laura's White House. Due to a number of strokes she had suffered, Lady Bird could no longer speak and was in a wheelchair, but she smiled and teared up and clapped her hands when she saw employees she knew, furniture and artwork she remembered, and rooms she loved. Other guests that fall included Prince Charles and his wife Camilla and the Dalai Lama.

For George's second term, Laura knew what she wanted to work on. She observed that the nation did not recognize the particular problems of boys—who dropped out of school more than girls, had more learning disabilities, were less likely to go to college, and were far more likely to go to jail or to get into trouble for drug and alcohol use. As adults, these boys did not know how to be fathers to their own children. So, Laura initiated the Helping America's Youth program. She saw to it that federal agencies worked together to serve young people. Particularly, she worked on aiding at-risk youth, such as those involved in gang violence and those who had gone to prison. She gathered activists from across the nation to share ideas about ways of helping these young men. She even invited to the White House former gang members and youth who had been to prison and who then went on to change their lives for the better. She wanted them to know, she said, "that they were welcome in the most prominent home in the nation."

Mrs. Bush sits with students at the Germantown Boys and Girls Club, Philadelphia, Pennsylvania, February 2005. Courtesy of George W. Bush Presidential Library.

Laura also addressed the problem of malaria, which was as deadly throughout the world as AIDS. The Bushes held the White House Summit on Malaria, which generated the same worldwide medical attention that had previously been brought to AIDS. Thousands of lives again were saved.

About the same time, Laura, at a White House cocktail party before the Kennedy Center Honors program for the arts, discovered that she and three other women were wearing the same red Oscar de la Renta dress, so Laura raced upstairs and changed into a black lace dress. That clothing faux pas received as much attention from the press as the malaria program.

Shortly thereafter, Laura learned that heart disease was the leading cause of death for women, and she decided to channel the outsized media attention that her red Oscar de la Renta dress received toward a worthy cause. The garment ended up traveling across the country, as part of the Heart Truth Red Dress campaign, to raise women's awareness of heart disease.

Her medical philanthropy didn't end there. She also became an advocate for women coping with breast cancer and embarked on programs with groups like MD Anderson Cancer Center to help women throughout the world.

Laura just kept making connections between seemingly unrelated events and seeking to help the world: from Africa, AIDS, and malaria to red dresses, heart disease, and breast cancer. She could always see a way to add a next step and change the world for the better.

For the rest of George Bush's presidency, he received both harsh criticism and loving prayers. Many Americans criticized him for the war in Iraq. When he began a "surge" in 2007 by sending twenty thousand more troops to that country, many people condemned him. This was a lonely time for the president, though Laura called it "one of his bravest moments in office." Yet, the judgment George endured was often personal and had nothing to do with his foreign or domestic policies. It was simply mean. But at the same time, a group called the First Lady's Prayer Group, which had been created by Susan Baker (the wife of George's father's Secretary of State James Baker) during the Clinton administration, prayed for George and Laura each week and sent them encouragement, as did a number of people from across the country.

After a few months, the much-decried surge in Iraq began to bear fruit. Violence had declined markedly, as had attacks on US troops. By the time the Bushes left office, Laura believed, she said, that "the loneliest of George's decisions, the surge, had been the right choice."

2008, George's last year in office, brought about a wedding and much travel. In February, Laura made her last trip to Africa and, in March, her last trip to Haiti. In April, Benedict XVI made the first visit of a pope to the White House in nearly thirty years. He said that he came on his birthday because "you spend your birthday with your friends."

In May, Jenna married Henry Hager at the Bush ranch in Crawford, surrounded by bluebonnets and pink evening primroses. The next month, Laura and George hosted a reception for them at the White House.

After the Hagers left on their honeymoon, Laura and George went one last time to the Middle East: Israel, Saudi Arabia, and Egypt. In June, Laura returned to Afghanistan and Slovenia, and in August she visited Burma, South Korea, and Thailand, even making a stop at the Beijing Olympics.

Wanting a smooth transition for the next president, the Bushes saw to it that the Obama staff had detailed information about how things were done, both at the White House and in Homeland Security, national security, economic policy, commerce and trade, and everywhere there would be a new team. President Bush met with President-elect Barack Obama in the Oval Office, Laura took Michelle Obama through the White House, and Jenna and Barbara showed Sasha and Malia where they would be living. The Bush girls advised the Obama girls that they should slide down the banister every once in a while just because they could.

Laura wrote the following about her memories of being First Lady:

> In the White House, George and I had hosted over fifteen hundred social events; many were to award medals or honor accomplishments of great moments in American arts and literature. . . . I had started the National Book Festival, which now draws some 120,000 visitors each fall, and I had worked to combat illiteracy worldwide. I had done what I had hoped to do: I had worked to be a good steward of the White House for our nation. Every day, even the difficult ones, had been a privilege.

Former First Ladies Barbara and Laura Bush discuss their time in the White House at the LBJ Presidential Library, Austin, Texas, November 2012.

Mrs. Bush visits an elementary school for United Way Reading Day, Dallas, Texas, March 2024. Courtesy of George W. Bush Presidential Library.

CHAPTER 5

RETIREMENT

George and Laura headed back home to Texas. They stopped first in Midland, where thirty thousand cheering people awaited them on the downtown square. "The presidency," said George, "was a joyous experience, but nothing compares with Texas at sunset." They made it home to the ranch, where it was dark and quiet and had no staff to unpack their bags or sharpshooters to protect them. They were back with the wildflowers and coyotes howling, sagebrush and cicadas buzzing—the place they loved.

Soon they began planning their presidential library and working on a new house in Dallas, where they would split their time with the ranch. Their schedule remained unrelenting, with speaking engagements and charitable events—from the Salvation Army to the new National Museum of African American History and Culture. "There is much meaning and purpose," Laura said, "to be found in a post-presidential life." Added to their projects was the joy of watching their daughters marry, pursue careers, and have grandchildren for them to adore.

And Laura, of course, continued to look for ways to help other people, as she had done throughout her life.

SELECTED BIBLIOGRAPHY

Bush, Laura. *Spoken from the Heart*. Scribner, 2010.

Hager, Jenna Bush, and Barbara Pierce Bush. *Sisters First*. Grand Central Publishing, 2017.

Hummer, Jill Abraham. *Laura Bush: Texas Roots, Global Impact*. University Press of Kansas, 2025.

Kessler, Ronald. *Laura Bush: An Intimate Portrait of the First Lady*. Doubleday, 2006.

www.ingramcontent.com/pod-product-compliance
Lightning Source LLC
LaVergne TN
LVHW041530141125
825302LV00015B/60
9781477332115